SON OF A HIGHLANDER

SON OF A
HIGHLANDER

ALISTAIR MACLEOD

Library of Congress Control Number:		2015918893
ISBN:	Hardcover	978-1-5144-4281-4
	Softcover	978-1-5144-4280-7
	eBook	978-1-5144-4279-1

Print information available on the last page.

Rev. date: 12/11/2015

To order additional copies of this book, contact:
Xlibris
1-800-455-039
www.Xlibris.com.au
Orders@Xlibris.com.au
727778

CONTENTS

This book is dedicated to the memory of my late father Harry Bliss MacLeod, a man who was extremely proud of his Scottish Highland heritage.

CHAPTER ONE

Introduction -The Story - Discovery

Introduction

The Story

When I was a small boy, my father would sit me down and tell me of the family story—of who I am and where my bloodline came from. He would say to me, 'You are a Mac Leod. The *Mac* is Gaelic and means *Son of*. The *Leod* is a Norse name, derived from the Vikings who settled in far western Scotland. Our ancestry home is "The Isle of Skye".' He explained that the family originated from a small acreage near Dunvegan Village. He would tell me of the clan feuds with the neighbouring clan, the MacDonalds, whereby the bloody warfare lasted for over a hundred years. My father would tell me of the family being forced off their lands by the English. My great-great grandfather was Donald MacLeod, a master blacksmith on the island; he lived in Portree. Family legend tells how he fought in the American Civil War, and when he returned to Portree, he would light up his pipe using worthless American confederate notes (money) which he brought back from the war. He was known to be able to pick up the heavy blacksmith anvil and throw it a considerable distance.

Donald, with his family, migrated from Scotland to Australia, settling in Bunderberg, Queensland, around the 1880s. Donald's son Peter, my great-grandfather, travelled to Melbourne and went under an alias, and was killed at an early age in a trench accident. There were two types of tartans that hung in our family home, MacLeod of Harris and MacLeod of Lewis along with the clan's crest badge of a bull's head surrounded by a buckle with the tartan as the backdrop with the motto, 'Hold Fast'. My grandfather Jack MacLeod, a very successful businessman, built a Tudor home at Ascot Vale, Melbourne, overlooking the Maribynong River. This he affectionately named the House Dunvegan, after Dunvegan Castle, the seat of the MacLeod chieftains on the Isle of Skye.

Forty odd years later, I found myself sitting down with my own son Brandon and explaining to him the same story told to me by my father, of who he is and his forefathers, that we're Highlanders from the Isle of Skye. Here I was talking about Donald MacLeod, the master blacksmith, and his son Peter, who was killed tragically in a trench and who went under an alias name. There were many unanswered questions I wanted to know now. What had happened to Donald MacLeod, my great-great-grandfather? This Highlander had vanished from the records. And why did his son go under an alias? Ironically my grandfather, Peter's son, had kept in contact with his Scottish relations well after his father's death, those who stayed behind in Scotland when the family migrated to Australia. It was accepted in the family that there was some type of family fallout, being the reason Peter changed his name, and researching the Internet and documentation from ancestry links revealed the same reason was also given by others who were descendant of Peter. My father, who passed away many years ago, travelled to Bunderberg, Queensland, in the 1950s in search of the reasons for the alias and what had happened to Donald. He met with relations, but no one could bear any light on the story.

As a small boy, I was told by my grandmother, who had married the grandson of Donald MacLeod, how she experienced a ghostly apparition of Donald MacLeod coming to her room in an angry state, speaking in Gaelic with the image of his face, which she explained had a goatee beard, in the corner of the room. As a boy, I thought what nonsense, as I still do, but the story fascinated me. This Scottish Highlander, who somehow was from a family who were dispossessed from their lands in the far western Isles of Scotland, fought in the American Civil War, was a master blacksmith on the Isle of Skye, a wild disposition, a Gaelic-speaking person from a Highland clan, who had sailed to Australia in the 1880s and who had vanished around the same time his son was killed.

I was now in my midlife, and wanted to find out the truth behind the family story. And how far could I go back in the family tree, father to son. So I embarked on completing one of my late father's goals that was not achieved—finding out what had happened to Donald and discover for myself the truth of the family story handed down through generations regarding the family being dispossessed from their traditional lands. I embarked on what I can only describe as the biggest emotional journey of my life. It is believed by many people that either the environment or/and genetics make up who we become. How similar were my forefathers to me? Did they hold the same values as the likes of my father and I? What were their strengths and weaknesses? Did they have any kind of prosperity in their lives or were their lives totally about adversity? Tracing one's own history, one's own ancestry, can be the most gratifying and emotional journey one can take. Every one of us will have an incredible family history; many people just have not discovered theirs.

In my family possessions, I had a 1797 British coin. It had been handed down through generations of father to son. I had inherited an old tattered leather photo album that contained photos of my grandfather Jack, with correspondence to his cousins in Scotland during World War I. These where all Donald's grandchildren. Jack had fought with the 29th Battalion in France on the western front, the battle of Somme, Polygon Wood, and was wounded in Passchendaele. And there was an address at the back of one of these old photos. It was now nearly 100 years since this correspondence, and 131 years since Donald migrated to Australia. Was I able to find the grandchildren of my grandfather's cousins? What stories do they hold, who all share the same great-great grandfather.

I travelled to the Isle of Skye Scotland to discover and learn of what did exactly happen to my people. After much researching through ancestry records, from Australia and Scotland along with shipping records and meeting people from the Isle of Skye, Scotland, along with reading into the history of the Highlanders, I was able to answer the questions I had regarding the family.

Discovery

I made contact with an Alan Hawthorn by email from Scotland who we both have the same great-great-grandfather Donald. Ironically, Alan was brought up by his grandmother at the address written at the back of the 100-year-old postcard from my grandfather's collection.

I flew to Glasgow, Scotland, and met with Alan and Kathleen Hawthorn over lunch, we both produced family documentation, when Alan displayed a photo of my grandfather Jack taken nearly a hundred years ago in Melbourne, Australia, proving our connection beyond doubt. Alan also produced another photo of Anne MacLeod, his great-grandmother, my grandfather's auntie with two Australian soldiers which look like the 29th Battalion badges on their arms. My grandfather's mates meeting his Scottish auntie who had stayed behind when his grandfather migrated to Australia.

I travelled to the Isle of Skye, 131 years after my people had left. I was to knock on the door of a terrace house in Portree of which I had traced, being the home to that of my great-great-grandfather Donald. It was now a bed and breakfast, and I explained to the owner, 'My name is Alistair MacLeod. I am under the belief that this was the home of my great-great-grandfather.' To my shock, the owner named Charlotte said, 'That's correct, Alistair. He was the blacksmith Donald MacLeod. He lived here with his family, and his son Peter was the apprentice blacksmith.'

I was to spend the night in the home of my great-great-grandfather. I was to meet a local historian, a MacDonald, that would take me to the site of the blacksmith shop where I would meet the owner Lorne Nicholls, who took me to his farm near the Braes. He showed me the cast iron gates made from the blacksmith shop, most possibly by my great-great-grandfather, the master blacksmith 140 years ago.

During my time on the Isle, I had made contact with another family member, an Ian Kindt by email, introduced by Charlotte the owner of the once home of Donald MacLeod. Ian's grandparents migrated to Australia after the second world war. He shares the same great-great-grandfather Donald and had also visited Portree and also like me had knocked on the same house where the family had lived in the 1870s. His grandparents had made contact with my grandfather in 1920, and my father had stayed with his grandparents in Queensland, Australia, in the 1950s while trying to trace the story. Incredibly this chance connection with Ian enabled me to fill in the gaps of the story of Donald's other daughter Jessie, who at the last moment was afraid to sail on the dangerous voyage on the Renfrewshire sailing ship to Australia in 1882, and ran up the gang plank and stayed in Scotland. Donald and his three other children were never to see her again. Although generations of the family had stayed in contact, I was also able to finally find out what had happened to Donald, and the most likely the reason why Peter went under an alias. Donald went gold mining in northern Queensland, and was hospitalised only two weeks after the death of his only son. The authorities of the time in Queensland had a government policy for the destitute, **To be removed from the public eye.** Hence this master blacksmith, Scottish Highlander was now destitute and was taken to Stradbroke Island off Queensland and dumped at the Benevolent Asylum for the destitute. His only crime being, he was poor, and he survived eight years on the island. He eventually died on the island and was buried in a pauper's grave with another 8,500 poor souls, regarded as the biggest mass grave in Australia and is hardly written in our history book

Through extensive searching in Australia and by the assistance of the genealogy department in Portree on the Isle of Skye, I was able to trace back the family to the 1700s, father to son Highlanders, who were crofters on a small two-acre lot, who were dispossessed from their lands during the horrendous Highland clearances whereby these proud people, a once strong warrior race, were forced off their lands they had occupied for many generations and replaced by sheep in some cases. I was to learn that after the Battle of Culloden, the Scottish clan system, traditions, and culture were to be destroyed by the English authority. Their language of Gaelic was banned, they were forbidden to play bag pipes, and the tartan was outlawed. They were persecuted by the English and dispossessed from their country, no different in comparison with the horrendous treatment of the Australian Aboriginal or the American Indian. The clan system, along with their traditions and culture that was known throughout the islands and Highlands for 800 years in some cases, was to be no more. The Isle of Skye went from a population of 24,000 people to 4,000 by 1881. I traced back to as far as my great-great-great-great-grandfather, another Donald, who raised his son John on the small two-acre crofter plot, ironically John was born around the same time as the family coin dated 1797 was handed down now to my son, eighth generations of MacLeods.

I stood on a hill overlooking the cemetery of St Mary's church, now in ruins, that lies not far from Dunvegan Castle the stronghold of the MacLeod clan. On this hill is also the burial ground of the MacLeod clan. I looked down on the area of two acres that my people lived for possibly hundreds of years. In the cemetery, not a marker defines my people who lay here, although several MacLeod Chieftains were buried here, my people were not chieftain line, but they are buried here neither less in this region where they made their home for possibly hundreds of years. On the death certificates of Donald, John, and Donald senior, the word **PAUPER** has been written. All these men lived lives of adversity, overcoming insurmountable obstacles. My grandfather Jack would also experience adversity and a horrendous life experience in the western front, where a million people lost their lives and 47,000 Australian soldiers died. He was wounded and regarded as one of the lucky ones. He continued seeking information regarding his Scottish Highland origin and making contact with his people.

There are pinnacles in one's life, some are joyous some or not, but they define who we are, for example, to witness the birth of your son or being there at the death of your father. Moments of one's life—both joy and pain—that define your character. Standing on the burial grounds of the MacLeod clan, looking over the two acres my family lived on for many of generations was another pinnacle in life, an emotional moment. One hundred and thirty-one years after they left the Isle of Skye, I had returned to discover who I am, and it hit me emotionally what my father had been drumming into me all those years ago. I had also overcome insurmountable obstacles in my life to achieve my dreams and accomplish my ambitions, but life's not about prosperity, it's about adversity and overcoming any insurmountable obstacle that life places in front of you. At this moment, on that hill on the Isle of Skye, Scotland, the other side of the world from my home in Australia, I discovered who I really was. It was what my father had been telling me as a boy, you are a MacLeod, Mac meaning *Son of*. Now I really understood and felt this enormous connection and understanding of my forefathers' lives. Everyone has a family story; this is my story, of father to son for over 200 years. I am the Son of these men, incredible people who lived incredible lives: father to son of eight generations: SON OF A HIGHLANDER. My family's story.

CHAPTER TWO

History of Clan MacLeod - The Holy Grail of the Clan
(The Fairy Flag) - MacLeod's Tables

History of the Clan MacLeod 1200–1500

The name Clan MacLeod was derived from a Gaelic term *Mac,* meaning *Son* originally being Clann Mhic Leoid. The Leod comes from an old Norse name Ljodhhus, common belief in MacLeod tradition is Leod was the son of Olaf the Black, King of the Isle of Mann and a large part of the Hebrides. This king of Viking ruled the Isle of Mann and part of the Hebrides around 1200s AD. Clan means *children* in Gaelic or *family,* so Clan MacLeod means *The Children of the Son of Leod,* or the family of the son of Leod. Clan MacLeod's origins were derived from both Celtic and Viking bloodlines. Leod held country in the inner and outer Hebrides of Uist, Harris, Lewis and a large part of the Isle of Skye. He died in 1280 and was buried on the holy island of Iona, where six successive chiefs of the clan were buried.

Leod had two sons, Tormod and Torquil. By virtue of these two sons inheriting different lands, this led to the creation of two branches of the clan that both lay claim being descendant from Leod who ruled in the thirteenth century. Tormod founded Siol

Thormoid and occupied the lands of Harris and part of Skye, creating MacLeod of Harris and Skye known as MacLeod of Harris and Dunvegan being MacLeod of MacLeod. Torquil founded Soil Torquil and occupied the Isle of Raasay and lands of Lewis, creating MacLeod of Lewis and Raasay. My ancestry was traced to the Clan MacLeod of MacLeod known as MacLeod of Dunvegan on the Duirinish Pennisula on the Isle of Skye.

The Isle of Skye is renowned as a mystical Island, with history steep in legend and folklore of feuding clans and bloody battles. It is arguably one of the most scenic places on Earth—mist enshrouded mountains, some with jagged peaks, velvet moors, and the sparkling water of lochs with towering rocky cliffs. It has been suggested that the name Isle of Skye may have been derived from the Norse word **Ski** meaning cloud and the **Ey** meaning island. The traditional Gaelic name is **An t-Eilean Sgitheananch** in Gaelic *Sgitheanach* describes a winged shape there is no definitive agreement as to the name's origin. Or *Eilean a' Cheò*, which means *island of the mist* is a poetic Gaelic name for the island.

The entire island of Skye comprises approximately 350,000 acres and is 7 miles to 25 miles broad and 50 miles long with 350 miles of rugged coastline, and is the largest island out of 67 in Scotland. The Cuillin, a volcanic mountain range, with its mystical magic quality, rises above 1,000 metres and can be seen throughout the Island with its eleven peaks over nine miles long.

The seat of the Chief of Clan MacLeod is Dunvegan Castle, the oldest consecutive castle lived in Scotland, some of the castles earliest building dated back to the thirteenth century when occupied by Leod. Eight hundred years of consecutive of being occupied by the chieftains of the MacLeod of MacLeod. With this 800-year-old history, records have been kept regarding the clan from song to legendary stories, and the collection of clan relics.

The Holy Grail of the Clan

The Fairy Flag

Within the walls of Dunvegan Castle is the Clan MacLeod's prized possession, the fairy flag. It is a silk flag that is protected in a frame, tattered and torn with many pieces missing. There are several stories of the flag's origin. Known as the *fairy flag*, MacLeod legend tells the story of a MacLeod chieftain who had married a fairy princess. After twenty years she was forced to leave him and return to fairyland. At the fairy bridge three miles from the castle, she said goodbye and the fairy princess gave the flag to her husband. The flag was said to have magical properties and can protect the MacLeod clan three times only. Folklore states it has been used two times already, once to win a battle against another rival clan, of which it was waved and the MacLeod Clan appeared to double in numbers to the enemy. Another time it was used to stop an epidemic, which threatened the starvation of the clan. In modern times, it was offered by the MacLeod chieftain to stand atop of the cliffs of Dover and wave the flag in the event of a German invasion.

Experts have dated the flag between the fourth and seventh centuries AD. The fabric is silk, and may have come from the Middle East, as one theory is a connection with the crusades, the religious war when Christian Knights waged war against the Muslims in Jerusalem in an attempt to reclaim the Holy Land. But if the experts are right with the dating, the flag could be 400 years older than this crusade theory. Another theory is, it could be the robe of an early Christian saint. or the Viking origin being a war banner of King Harald Haardrade of Norway, killed in 1066, from whom Olaf the Black, King of Mann and part of the Hebrides were said to have descended.

When I visited Skye in 2013, I asked the question regarding the legend of the fairy flag to locals during a night at the Dunvegan tavern. I was drinking whisky with several locals and was told by a fisherman, with a broad Scottish accent that:

'There is [sic] actually people who really believe they see the fairies every two months in the rocky knolls on the hills close to the village, he went on to laugh at these so-called sightings, as he explained to me, how could this possibly be so, witnessing the fairies every two months, he continued laughing, I've lived here all my life and I only see the fairies every two years, not every two months.'

MacLeod's Tables

In 1536, Alasdair Crotach MacLeod the eighth MacLeod chieftain who had obtained his name Crotach, meaning *humpbacked* in Scottish Gaelic, due to receiving a blow to his back in a broad sword fight with a MacDonald that left him with the back injury, hence, the name humpbacked. Alasdair had visited Holyrood palace in Edinburgh, and had boasted that his banqueting hall at Dunvegan was much grander than that of Holyrood palace. King James IV some time later after the MacLeod chieftain's boasting, arrived on the Isle of Skye. Alasdair instead of taking the king to Dunvegan castle, where his empty boasting would be exposed, he took the king to the top of a nearby flat-topped mountain. He had arranged for hundreds of MacLeod clansmen to hold flaming torches to light up the open air, he had also arranged an almighty feast in the open air. MacLeod legend has it that this MacLeod chieftain told the king:

'Welcome, Sire, to my banqueting hall, its floor the mighty deep, its roof the canopy of heaven. My table is 2,000 feet high and here bearing the lighted torches are your loyal servants.'

Hence, the area is now known as MacLeod's Tables. King James IV rewarded Alasdair Crotach lands on Skye that the MacDonald clan claimed to be their possession. This caused conflict between the clans and may be the main reason behind the 100-year war with the MacDonalds; a policy of divide and rule created by King James IV.

CHAPTER THREE

Bloody Battles of the Clan - The Battle of the Spoiling Dyke -
The War of the One-eyed Woman - Feasting and Drinking -
Pen Now Mightier than the Broad Sword

Bloody Battles of the Clans

Scotland is renowned for feuding clans and bloody warfare throughout the islands and highlands. The bloodiest of continuing feud among all clans is that of the continuation of more than 100 years of battle between MacLeod and MacDonald clans on the Isle of Skye and neighbouring Islands.

In 1577, history tells a tale of members of the MacLeod clan, who were turned away from the Island of Eigg by the Clan MacDonald of Clanranald also known as Clan Ranald. MacLeod tradition tells of a party of MacLeod men that landed on the Island in a hungry desperate state, and were denied food. Some were killed by the occupiers, and three were left to drift in a boat out to sea with their hands tied. A MacDonald theory is the MacLeod men had mistreated their women when they arrived on the island. But what is known as fact is that fellow MacLeods who were fishing, accidently stumbled across the desperate fellow clansmen drifting in the misty waters and perishing in their boats, hands tied by the occupants of the Isle of Eigg. Hellbent on revenge, the MacLeod chieftain

Alasdair Crotach MacLeod sailed with a large party of warriors to the Isle of Eigg. The inhabitants of approximately 400 people had hidden in a cave on the seashore of the island, when the party of MacLeod warriors landed on their island for revenge. Extensive searching did not uncover the 400 population that were well hidden inside the cave. The MacLeods left the island and noticed a person standing high on a hilltop, watching them sailing away. They quickly returned to the shoreline and climbed the hill where they were able to track the person's footprints in the snow, which led them to the cave where the 400 inhabitants were hiding. A bonfire was built at the entrance of the cave from all the heath and vegetation nearby and lit, with the fire and smoke killing the entire population of Eigg of 400 people.

The Battle of the Spoiling Dyke

In 1578, another battle took place between the MacLeod and the MacDonald clans that may well have been a revenge for the massacre the previous year on the Isle of Eigg. The MacDonalds of Uist, located west over the water from Trumpan on the Isle of Skye in what is known as the outer Hebrides, landed on the shores of Admore Bay, Isle of Skye, on the Waternish peninsula and surrounded the Trumpan church. Members of the MacLeod clan where inside the stone building and thatched roof, conducting a church service being a Sunday, when the church was set on fire with nearly the entire group of worshipers killed, by either fire and suffocation or being cut down with the broad sword as they tried to escape. The only survivor was a young girl who managed to escape and give the alarm. The MacLeods were able to quickly dispatch their boats and sailed and rowed to Trumpan, where they found the MacDonalds trying to get their boats back into the water, that had been caught on the high tide. The MacLeods slaughtered every MacDonald and collected all their corpses and laid them along a rocky dyke (fence) and pushed the rocky dyke over onto the dead. History tells of the bones of the dead MacDonalds protruding through the rocks of the dye for many years after the event. It became known as the Battle of the Spoiling Dyke. Gaelic Scottish Blar Milleadh a' Gharaidh Millegearaidh.

The War of the One-eyed Woman

The last of the battles between the two rivalling clans and, in my opinion, the most bizarre battle, took place in 1601; it has become known as the war of the one-eyed woman. In Gaelic, it is known as The **Battle of Coire na Creiche.** The MacLeod Chieftain Rory Mor MacLeod attempted to make peace with the MacDonalds and offered the hand of his sister in marriage to the Chieftain Donald Gorm Mor MacDonald. The terms of the marriage was known as a handfast arrangement, where by the man and the woman live together as man and wife for up to a year and a day, and during this time if the woman gave birth to a male child to be her heir, then the marriage would happen. If a male child was not produced, then no marriage would take place. After the year and the day period had taken place, the MacLeod woman had not given birth to a child whatsoever, thus Donald MacDonald sent her back to the MacLeod clan with the most bizarre of insults. He had discovered she was blind in one eye, and tied her facing backward, onto a one-eye horse, led by a one-eyed servant and followed along by a one-eyed mongrel dog, back to Dunvegan castle to her brother Chieftain Rory MacLeod.

This insult resulted in a revenge that became the last battle of the two warring clans, whereby hundreds of clansmen died from both sides, and a creek on which they fought became known as 'little red river' as it was said the blood of the dead ran like a river for days. This was not just the last clan battle of the feuding MacLeods and MacDonalds but the last battle of feuding clans in the entire Scotland.

Feasting and Drinking

After the battle of the one-eyed woman, the King of England intervened and forced both the MacLeods and MacDonalds to a ceasefire agreement. After the agreement was signed by both Chieftains, Rory MacLeod hosted three weeks of feasting and drinking of wine at Dunvegan castle, whereby the MacDonalds were their guests and a once enemy to the MacLeod clan had become newfound friends. The MacLeod chieftain had the MacLeods heredity bagpipers the MacCrimmons compose a bagpipe tune that remembered the 100 years of feuding of the two clans and was played as the piper led the MacDonald clan into the castle at Dunvegan for three weeks of feasting and drinking.

Pen Now Mightier than the Broad Sword

In 1609, King James, who was then King of Scotland, Ireland, and England, created what is known as the statutes of Iona. This law was created to force a once fighting warrior race into being farmers or fisherman. King James was strapped for cash and was wanting the Highlands to be productive in farming or fishing and creating a law stopping a culture of feuding and feasting. This was the reason behind the statutes of Iona, whereby chieftains were forced to sign a series of acts or face imprisonment. A common belief is the Highlanders were considered to be barbaric and uncivilised by the English, and the series of legal acts were an attack on the Gaelic culture, Anglicising or de Gaelic zing.

Amongst the provisions of the statutes were that the Highland Chieftains send their heirs to the lowlands of Scotland to be educated in English speaking.

- The provision and support of Protestant ministers to Highland Parishes
- The establishment of hostelries

- The outlawing of beggars
- The prohibition of traditional hospitality and strong drink
- Limitations on the bearing and use of arms
- The outlawing of bards and other bearers of the traditional culture
- The prohibition on the protection of fugitives

As a result of these new laws, the MacLeod and MacDonald clans adopted a new religion. This was the start of what many people believe was a Government aim at destroying the Scottish Highlands traditional culture by law.

The once powerful warlord Rory MacLeod and all other Highland chieftains had now become curtailed by King James, and the statutes of Iona was the beginning of the end of the clan system that had survived for centuries.

The writer Alistair MacLeod standing on the hill above the burial grounds of the MacLeod Clan with the MacLeod Tables as the back drop. Within 1 km of this spot was the 2-acre family home.

Kilmuir the burial grounds of the MacLeod Clan, along with the ruins of the church.

A replica of a Crofter Black house on the Duirinish Peninsula Isle of Skye, the family home on the 2-acre crofter plot at Kilmuir would have been similar to the one pictured.

Dunvegan Castle, the seat of the MacLeod Clan.

The 1797 King George 111 penny coin, handed down through the generations of MacLeods

The MacLeod Crest - Badge with the buckle and motto written: HOLD FAST

Clan territories of The Isle of Skye & neighbouring islands.

CHAPTER FOUR

Donald MacLeod senior 1700s - The
Penny Coin - Battle of Culloden

Donald MacLeod Senior
Mid to late 1700s

D onald MacLeod senior was my great-great-great-great-grandfather. He lived on a small two-acre crofter plot within half a mile of the eastern shoreline of Lock Dunvegan. The area is called Kilmuir, which would be Dunvegan village today, between Kilmuir road and the primary school. This is the location of where generations of MacLeods were raised. A short walking distance from the two acres is the ruins of St Mary's Church Kilmuir, known originally as the Parish Church for Duirinish. It is now a roofless church dating back to 1694. It has now become the burial place of the MacLeod Chieftains since 1835 where six consecutive Chieftains were buried within the walls of the roofless church. Previous to St Mary's as a burial place, Chieftains were buried at Rodel, Isle of Harris, where Alasdair Crotach Tomb is, as Harris at the time was the spiritual place of the clan, and Dunvegan was the seat of the Chiefs. And in the beginning the burial grounds of the Chieftains were the Holy Isle of Iona, where Leod was buried in 1280 and other five successive chieftains followed.

But it's in the area near the burial grounds of the MacLeod clan at St Mary's Church Kilmuir on the Isle of Skye where I trace my family's lineage, the home of my people, on a small two-acre crofter plot within a mile of these burial grounds of the MacLeod Chieftains. Not a marker defines the burial spot of my ancestors as they were not chieftains or heredity pipers, as many generations of the MacCrimmons bag pipers, for the MacLeod chieftains were also buried there on this sacred ground. My family would have had a stone or a wooden cross that has been lost in time for their burial marker. But they were buried here nevertheless; they were born and raised here, and their families died in this area, for possibly many generations on this ground. I have traced four generations of my ancestors living here and at nearby Portree.

Donald MacLeod senior	John MacLeod	Donald MacLeod	Peter MacLeod
b 1700s	b 1797	b 1834	b 1866

The Penny Coin

Donald MacLeod senior was a crofter who raised a family on the small two-acre crofter plot. He married a Catherine Bain, and they had two children that I know of—a son, John MacLeod, born around 1797, and a daughter Anne. Ironically the coin handed down to me from father to son is a 1797 British coin. The coin is a penny of King Georg 111 era. Was this coin a token on the birth of Donald's son John or a kept token from a baptism? I will never know the truth but it has been handed down through my generation father to son and now to the eighth generation, my son Brandon.

The 1797 King George 111 penny coin handed
down through generations of MacLeods

The mid- to late 1700s was going to be a very difficult time for
the Scottish Highlanders, in particular the date of 1747 stands out
in the Scottish history more than any other. This was the date of
the ill-fated Battle of Culloden of which the Highland clan system,
culture, and traditions were to change forever.

Battle of Culloden and the Jacobites, 1746

On the island of Eriskay, in the outer Hebrides in 1745, landed the
then 23-year-old Prince Charles Edward Stuart, to be known as
Bonnie Prince Charlie (The Young Pretender). He was the French-
born grandson of King James VII of Scotland and II of England and
Ireland. His grandfather was overthrown from his throne in 1689.
The catholic King James fled to France in exile. The word Jocobite
comes from the Latin word James. It was coined as the exiled King
and his supporters refused to accept the coup that had taken place,
hence, the name 'The Pretender' was inherited by the former King
and his son James Francis Edward Stuart, and later to his grandson
Bonnie Prince Charlie. Since the 1689 coup against the Catholic
King occurred and the dreaded day of 1747 (The Battle of Culloden),

five Jacobite uprisings have taken place. These uprisings had the assistance of some of the clans of the Scottish Highlands and the support of the French and also once with the Spanish.

Bonnie Prince Charlie landed on Eriskay with only seven men and was advised from the Highlanders who greeted him to go home; his reply was 'I am home.' Within the month, Bonnie Prince Charlie had convinced some Chieftains of the Isles and mainland to assist in the fifth Jacobite uprising, and gained the support of 1,200 clansmen from several clans. Recruitment continued and by the time Bonnie Prince Charlie reached Holyrood house taking Edinburgh, his army was believed to have reached 2,500 Jacobites. This number doubled to 5,000 when the Jacobite army marched into England taking Carlisle, Preston, Lancaster, and Manchester.

The French were supposed to have invaded England and assist the Jacobite cause. But no form of communication from his French allies was received, creating doubt with the Jacobites if they did have the assistance of the French at all. But notice was received about the Duke of Cumberland, the King's son, was arranging an attack on the Jacobites with a larger army. This army force of redcoats were also called Hanoverians. The Highlander leaders who were uncomfortable of continuing to London decided on a tactical withdrawal that would be in the best interest of the Jacobites. So as a result of the withdrawal, 5,000 clansmen tramped back to Scotland with Cumberland's army in hot pursuit. On February 1746, three months since taking Manchester England, the Jacobite army was now back in the Highlands of Scotland. By April 1746, the Jacobites were exhausted from fighting and tramping through the winter snows. Their numbers had now reached over 6,000 of which most were exhausted and hungry.

On the Drummossie Moor at Culloden house near Inverness, on the 16th of April 1746, the bloodiest of battles of all the Jacobite uprisings occurred, and the last battle fought on British soil began. Close to 13,000 men from both sides, battled out in what is considered to be a civil war. It was not a war of English against the Scottish, it has been reported and contested that there was more Scott's fighting for the Hanovien side than the Jacobites. Highlander against lowlanders, highlanders against highlanders. There where cases of family against another family member. Some fought for the Stuarts to rule, believing in the Prince, others believed in fighting against the English, others were forced to fight for their chieftain's request, or would be evicted from their crofter plots, others wanted a return of Catholic rule to the throne, and others were loyal to their clan. The MacLeod of MacLeod and MacDonald of Sleat had hundreds of clansmen meet at Baracadale to fight for the Jacobites but were told to return home by both chieftains and did not fight at Culloden, but 120 MacLeod's from the Isle of Raassay fought at Culloden with the Jacobites alongside Clan MacLachlan. Bonnie Prince Charlie had chosen the rough, marshy moor to fight; this choice was opposed by his Commanding Officer Lord George Murray, who believed this choice of location was detrimental to the Jacobites whose main weapon was 'The Highland Charge', A historical account of the Highland Charge is as follows:

'The charge required a high degree of commitment as the men were rushing into musket range and would suffer casualties from at least one volley. Speed was essential to the charge, so the Highlanders preferred to employ the charge downhill and over firm ground; they removed clothing from their lower body for the same reason. They ran forward in clusters of a dozen (often blood relatives) which formed a larger wedge shaped formation. Once in effective musket range (60 yards) those with firearms would shoot; gun-smoke from this mass discharge having obscured enemies' aim, the Highlanders obtained further protection from the expected return volley from the opposing force by crouching low to the ground immediately after firing. Then, firearms were dropped and edged weapons drawn, whereupon the men made the final rush on the enemy line uttering Gaelic yells. On reaching striking distance the Highlander would attempt to take the opponent's sword or bayonet point on his targe while lunging in low to deliver an upward thrust to his enemy's torso.'

Despite Murray's protest, Bonnie Prince Charlie, being the Commander in Chief, insisted on this terrible location, and as a result by 4.00 pm on the 16th of April 1746, 1,500 Jacobites lay dead on the boggy moor. Hanoverians numbers were in the vicinity of 250, but the spilling of blood was not going to stop on the boggy marsh on that fatal day.

Cumberland appropriately became known as 'The Butcher'; he showed no mercy to the wounded. They were left to die where they lay on the moor and had his redcoats collect valuables from the dead and the dying. The killing continued with Cumberland's army committing atrocities against the Highland people. Stories of dozens of clansmen burnt alive while sheltering in a barn that was torched. Cumberland's soldiers executed many clansmen sheltering in Culloden house. Redcoats where sent into the Glens and hills to hunt down the Jacobites. Raiding parties over the next several months burnt down highlanders homes, killed the Jacobites by bayonet or musket. Others were hanged or burnt in their homes. Throughout the Highlands and Islands. Catholic Churches where destroyed Highlanders wife's and children where ravished. Entire townships where Highland people lived were destroyed. Thousands of head of cattle were taken from the clan. Several thousand people where gaoled, and many deported. Cumberland himself 'The Butcher' supervised this slaughter for several months after the ill-fated battle.

On the Isle of Raasay, the MacLeod's that had taken side with Jacobites had their homes torched and stock confiscated or destroyed, and were evicted from their lands. It is believed 300 homes were torched, and hundreds of sheep and cattle were killed.

And the Bonnie Prince Charlie, well, he did not stand and fight to the death as many of his Highlander supporters did on that fateful day. The Pretender fled to the Outer Hebrides and was assisted by Flora MacDonald who rowed him across the water to Skye. Dressed as a maid as a disguise, he hid in a sea shore cave for six days until a French sailing vessel rescued him, and he returned to France and never stepped on Scotland shores again.

CHAPTER FIVE

Skye Boat Song - The Disarming Act -
The Crofter System - The Highland Clearances

Skye Boat Song

The boat song is one of the Scottish Highland's most romantic and played songs, either recited as a poem, sung as a song, or theme played with a variety of musical instruments. Originally co-penned by a MacLeod woman who was being rowed over to Loch Coruisk on Skye, in Scottish Gaelic Coire Uisg the cauldron of waters is an inland freshwater loch at the foot of the Black Cuillin mountains. When the Highlander rowers broke into a Gaelic song while rowing, the song 'Cuachag nan Craobh' (The Cuckoo in the Grove). The song was letter penned adding the Jacobite association, and is the story of the escape of Prince Bonnie Charlie after Culloden with the assistance of Flora MacDonald.

> [Chorus:] Speed, bonnie boat, like a bird on the wing
> Onward! the sailors cry;
> Carry the lad that's born to be King
> Over the sea to Skye.

Loud the winds howl, loud the waves roar.
Thunderclouds rend the air;
Baffled, our foes stand by the shore,
Follow they will not dare.

Disarming Act

Any Highland chieftain that assisted the Jacobite cause was
stripped of their estates, removing any jurisdiction they once had.
The Disarming Act was created by the Crown of which a law was
created banning clansmen from carrying of any weapon's claymore
(broadsword) or muzzle. The Act prevented the Highlanders from
wearing kilts and displaying tartans, and even banned the playing of
the bag pipes. This was the beginning of the end for the Highland
Clans, and there was more atrocities installed for these once
proud clans, the Crown was about to not just destroy the culture
and traditions of a race of people, they were about to remove the
people themselves from the Islands and Highlands of Scotland, the
infamous Highland clearance was about to begin.

The Crofter System

Crofters are tenants who pay for the right to live and farm a small
area of country. In my family's case their area was only two acres,
but other crofters could have up to fifty acres. Prior to the word
crofter, clansmen would be granted a section of country to live on
as subsistence farming by the chieftain who controlled the estate.
An area was provided to him for his service and loyalty to the
chieftain and would honour this by fighting for the chieftain when
called to battle. During the 1700 and 1800s, many chieftains had
moved south due to the statute of Iona and for a more comfortable
existence. Being strapped for cash or for taxes owed to the Crown,
their estates were either sold or leased out to relatives, friends, or

wealthy sheep breeders of the south being from the lowlands of Scotland or England. These new tenants sub-leased to the existing once clansmen, and in most cases, keeping the productive country for themselves; whereby the original inhabitants were forced to survive on poorer soils or be evicted as became the case for thousands of people during the notorious Highland clearances.

The Highland Clearances

Donald MacLeod senior lived in terrible times. He was raised in the aftermath of the Battle of Culloden and experienced the horrendous treatment of his people during the Highland clearances and Government acts that tried to destroy the traditions and culture of the Highland clan system. He experienced the hardships of survival on a small two-acre piece of land, a semi-subsistence living.

Crofters where then being replaced by sheep from the south, removed from the country where they had lived for generations. People were evicted from their homes, the ones that stayed were forced onto small acreage which may be the case with my family or to unproductive land along the coast. This clearance of the people of the islands and highlands was to last for 140 years. The Isle of Skye was believed to have had a population in excess of 25,000 people in the late 1700s, and by the late 1800s had been reduced to 4,000 due to the Highland clearances. Horrendous stories were told of crofters being evicted from their lands, entire villages being destroyed, and people replaced by sheep, having their homes burnt to the ground, and families, women, and children forced into the snow-covered ground seeking shelter from other crofters who still had their homes. Violent evictions of people being chained and forced on to sailing vessels to the new worlds, dying of small pox and other diseases, confined to sailing ships that in some cases were not fit for merchants to move cargo, but were commissioned to move the Highlanders from their land.

CHAPTER SIX

John MacLeod 1797–1874 - Black House - Septs of
the Clan MacLeod - The Potato Famine - Donald
MacLeod 1834 –1908 - Master Blacksmith of Stormy
Hill - Marriage to Clan MacLeod of Lewis

John MacLeod
1797–1874

Black House

My great-great-great-grandfather was John MacLeod born around 1797. The only known son of Donald Senior, he was raised on the two-acre plot at Kilmuir. The homes of the crofters were known as Black Houses, a rough stone building with a thatched roof held down with stones tied at the bottom section of the thatching. The floor was an earth floor, and the centre of the home was a fire hearth for cooking and warmth. The smoke from the fireplace went straight into the thatched roof and slowly escapes. The northern side of the Isle had limited trees, therefore, limited wood fires. Most fires were created from peat that was cut from the earth carried back in a basket. A slow-burning material that would give off a smelly oily smoke, hence, the name black house. During the snowy winter period, livestock would be brought into the house, and one side of the black house consisted of cattle, geese, goats, sheep, etc., while the opposite side is where the family resided.

John married Anne MacKaskil from Uig, northeast of Dunvegan region and lies on the Trotternish peninsula. John was about 32 years of age and Anne only 20 when they married on the 9th of March 1829. The MacKaskills were septs to the Clan MacLeod. Other septs were as follows:

Septs of Clan MacLeod of Harris and Skye

Beaton (Betha, Bethea, Bethune, Beton).

Harold (Harald, Haraldson, Harrold, Herrald, MacHarold, MacRaild).

MacAndie (Andie, MacHandie, MacKande, MacKandy, Makcandy).

MacCaig (MacCoig, MacCowig, MacCrivag, MacCuaig, MacKaig, MacQuigg).

MacClure (MacAlear, MacClewer, MacLeur, MacLewer, MacLur, MacLure, McClure).

MacCrimmon (Cremmon, Crimmon, Grimmond, MacCrummen, MacGrimman, MacGrymmen
MacRimmon, MacCrimmon piping family)

MacWilliam (McCullie, MacKilliam, MacKullie, MacWilliams, MacWillie, MacWylie, Williamson.

Norman (Normand, Norval, Norwell, Tormud)

John and his wife raised three children on the same two acres where he was raised by his father Donald. Anne gave birth to Donald on the 12th February 1834, a daughter Catherine was born on the 12th July 1836, a second daughter Mary was born, then a Peter in 1837. Census in 1851 showed the family on their two-acre plot, Donald 17 was a farm labourer.

Potato Famine

Hardships continued during this era as the Isle of Skye and most of Scotland was to experience an extremely poor potato harvest. As with the likes of Ireland, the Isle of Skye had relied on the potato to support their diet. A potato blight overcame the crops during the 1830s to the 1850s. This was the time John and Anne were raising their young brood. Landowners of Skye lost income from tenants as no returns from their crops, hence, not being able to pay rents, forcing more of the crofters to leave the Isle, not to mention the starvation experienced by so many families. The twenty-fifth Chieftain Norman MacLeod of MacLeod of MacLeod was forced to leave Dunvegan Castle and live in London, as he could no longer provide work or food for his remaining tenants. It is during this time that a large part of the Clan MacLeod land was sold.

Census records of 1851 show the family's home was on their two-acre plot near Dunvegan, present John, 55; Anne, 43; Donald farm labourer, 17; Catherine, 13; Mary daughter present along with another son Peter, 8. So records indicate they survived the potato famine and Donald was labouring on the two acres. John died on 11 November 1874 at Kilmuir Parish of Duirinish in the county of Inverness, where the two-acre plot was located; he was aged 79. Written on his death certificate states '**Pauper**' formerly crofter, widow Anne Mackaskill, father Donald Crofter, deceased mother Catherine Bain, deceased sister Ann MacLeod signed the certificate with her mark a cross (**x**) crossed on the death certificate.

Donald MacLeod
1834–1908

Donald was my great-great-grandfather, and his life is of which has
driven me to write this book, experienced a remarkable Journey in
life, but not a fortunate one. Brought up on the two-acre Crofter plot
with his father working as a farm labourer at an early age. Donald
moved to Portree and married an Ann MacKaskill from Baracadale,
ironically the same name as his mother, they were both similar age.
His wife Anne was a Baracadale MacKaskill, parents being Kenneth
and Mary MacKaskill another Sept to the Clan MacLeod. They
had 6 children a daughter Mary born about 1857, Anne born 1859,
Peter my Great Grandfather born 7th June 1866, Jesse born 1868,
Flora born 1871 and Maggie Born 1874. Family legend has a story of
Donald lighting his pipe from worthless confederate money brought
back from America after the civil war. Many Scots fought over seas
as soldiers of fortune. As the American civil war offered a means to
an income, as many enlisted men had no means of earning money
to feed their family on the Isle. This may have been the case with

Donald desperate to feed his family he fought on foreign soil against an enemy he had no quarrel with. The 1861 census shows Anne with two of her daughters living with her brother at Baracadale, with no sign of Donald he may have been fighting in the American civil war at the time hence why Anne moved in with her Brother.

Donald was a master Blacksmith and smithies would have been in demand during the civil war in the United States. The war commenced in April 1861 when the Confederate Army bombarded Union soldiers at Fort Sumter South Carolina. The war ended in 1865 when Robert E Lee surrendered the last major Confederate Army to Ulysses S Grant. South Carolina had previously had many MacLeods migrate to this area during the Highland Clearance, either voluntarily or forcibly.

The Isle of Skye had a connection of the past with Carolina America, between 1732 and 1739. It has been alleged the eighth Chief of MacLeod along with the Chief of MacDonald of Sleat sold selected clan members as indentured servants to landowners in the Carolinas. The MacLeod chief was known as 'The Wicked Man'.

Master Black Smith of Stormy Hill

Donald lived at 39 Bayfield Portree, on the water's edge in one of the most scenic towns in Scotland. He was the assistant to Beaton, who had established a blacksmith shop on Stormy Hill, Portree. The 1871 census shows Donald at the Bayfield address, also Anne along with all six children. The Beaton families are Septs to the Clan MacLeod just like the MacKaskills, and Beaton was also raised in Kilmuir near Dunvegan. They may have been cousins or childhood friends. Stormy Hill overlooks the township with terrific views of the Cuillin Hills and Portree Loch. Beaton and MacLeod were master blacksmiths and skilled in wrought iron work, making of gates, cart wheels, etc.

Tragically Anne died of a heart attack on the 23rd of April 1879 at 43 years of age. She was buried only a short walk from where they lived in the Old Cemetery at Portree; not a marker defines the spot as it would have been a wooden cross that would have deteriorated over time.

Marriage to Clan MacLeod of Lewis

Donald was left to raise his four youngest children, his two eldest girls were 22 and 20 at the time, and most likely marrying and moved away at this stage. He married Christy MacLeod of the Isle of Raasay, who came from Clan MacLeod of Lewis branch of the MacLeods. This marriage took place on the Isle of Raasay on the 8th of June 1880, a year after the death of his wife. His son Peter became the apprentice blacksmith to his father on Stormy Hill and working with Beaton. Donald had moved to 5 Bossville terrace by the census of 1881. A two-storey terrace house with magnificent views looking over Loch Portree. He and his new wife Christy lived in one small room with all of the four remaining children. Also living at the premises were other three families. A tailor owned the house and lived with his family in one of the rooms; a fisherman with his family in another room; and a bagpiper and his family occupied the other room. Four families living under one roof, each family living in one room with all their children.

> 'On my trip to Skye at Portree I stayed the night in the once Home of Donald MacLeod at 5 Bossville Terrace of which now is a bed and breakfast, a local historian Norm MacDonald took me to the location of the Blacksmith shop. Lorne Nicholls, who resides at the site, took me to his farm at the braes where he had one of the original gates made in the era of my family at the Blacksmith shop, with a huge possibility it was made by my ancestor.' The local historian being a MacDonald commented on the quick marriage of Donald saying, "he was a MacLeod after all"?'

Census records 1851 showing John MacLeod & family residing on the 2 acre crofter plot at Kilmuir. Donald MacLeod was 17 years of age and was a farm labourer.

Death records of John MacLeod on the 11th of November 1874, his sister Anne MacLeod has signed the records by her signature being a cross of a mark

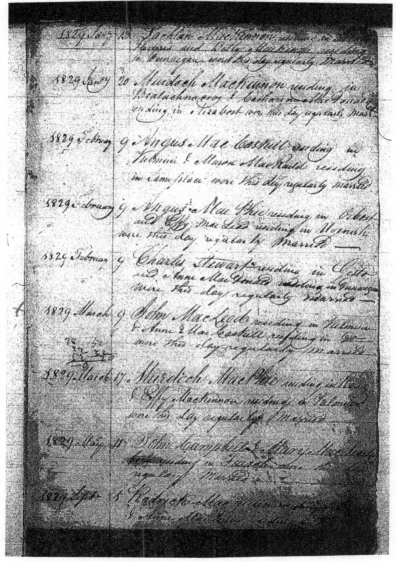

Marriage records of John MacLeod residing in Kilmuir marrying Anne
MacKaskill residing in Uig on the 9th of March 1829

Census records of Donald MacLeod and family living at Portree in 1871, occupation Blacksmith.

Portree Isle of Skye and harbour, Donald MacLeod and family lived in the now pinkish coloured terrace home over looking the harbour that can be seen in the photo in the 1870s to 1882.

MacLeod of Lewis Tartan

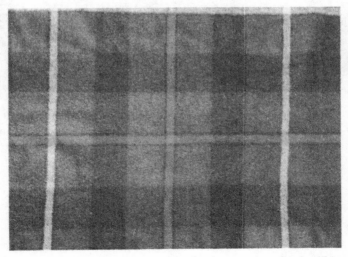

Hunting MacLeod Tartan as a blanket kept in swag [bed roll] by writer for 30 years.

Chapter Seven

The Voyage on the *Renfrewshire*, 1882 - Life at Sea

The Voyage on the *Renfrewshire*, 1882

In 1882, Donald left Portree and his island home where he and generations of MacLeods had lived for possibly hundreds of years. The Isle of Skye's population had fallen from 25,000 people to 4,000 due to the Highland clearances and the potato famine. The surviving Crofters in some cases had their rents increased by 30 per cent in one year. Even though Donald was a master blacksmith, work would have been limited due to the exodus of the island people. The Clyde steam boat was operating from Portree to Glasgow at this time, and more than likely this was the means the family reached Glasgow from where they would sail to Australia.

The *Renfrewshire* was one of the first iron hull built sailing ships, a merchant ship, built in the Port of Glasgow by Henry Murray and Company in 1875, and owned by Thomas Law & Company. A fully rigged ship of three masts, square rigged. She was 202.5 feet long; her beam was 33.1 feet; her depth was 20 foot. She carried four boats, only one as a life boat. She had at least three compasses, one in the pinnacle of which the vessel was steered. There was a standard compass on the fore deck and a tell-tale in the cabin skylight.

The *Renfrewshire.*

Donald and family boarded the *Renfrewshire* at the port at Lancaster, Glasgow, in June 1882. This dangerous voyage to Australia would take up to three months for a distance up to 13,750 nautical miles; destination was Bunderberg, Australia. At the very last moment, his daughter Jessie refused to participate in the voyage; she was only 16 years of age and may have stayed with her sister Anne in Glasgow. No information on the whereabouts of Donald's oldest daughter Mary, or whatever had happened to her, is known. Australian passenger records indicate only three of Donald's children migrated with him.

Donald Mcleod		Arrival Bunderberg	14th September 1882	Renfrewshire
Christy McLeod	wife	'' ''	'' ''	''
Peter McLeod	Son			
Flora McLeod	Daughter			
Maggie McLeod	Daughter			

The name MacLeod had been spelt with a **Mac** on all birth, marriage, Census and death certificates. The spelling with a **Mc** had been used with the likes of the shipping records and also with the signing of a name with a Mc.

Another MacLeod had made the voyage with them, a Murdock who was about 26 years of age; he may have been related to Christy. This was going to be the last time Donald and his three children would see Jessie or Ann again.

> 'In 1920, Jessie's Son John Paterson migrated to Australia, staying with his cousin Peter's son Jack MacLeod in Melbourne. Family story tells of Jack's baby son Harry being wet nursed by Paterson's wife Alice, who had the same age daughter. In the 1950s Harry visited the Paterson's who then lived in Queensland tracing the family story, ironically Paterson's grandson Ian Kindt and I have made contact by both visiting Skye and visiting the same home as Donald, both share the same great great grandfather, hence the story unfolds regarding Jessie refusing to sail to Australia.'

Peter was 16 years of age, his two sisters Flora 11 and Maggie 8 years of age. Deaths frequently occurred on these voyages caused by dysentery in a lot of cases. Infants and young children were very vulnerable. As many as one in five children, and one in sixty adults, died on these voyages to Australia. For burial, the body was sewn into a piece of canvas or placed in a rough coffin (often hastily knocked up by the ship's carpenter) and weighed down with pig iron or lead to help it sink. The sailing route was known as the 'Great Circle' or the Clipper way. This route from Glasgow caught the northeast trade winds of the Atlantic Ocean, would take ships to the equator known as the doldrums, where sailing vessels may be caught in a no-wind situation, causing them to lose up to three weeks of voyage time. Ships would continue south, sailing past west of Africa reaching 40 degree south known as the roaring forties. These strong prevailing winds that blew from the west would take sailing vessels passing far south of Cape of Good Hope in Southern Africa across the wild seas of the southern Indian Ocean then to Australian waters. Most captains prefers to sail around Tasmania than attempt to sail through Bass strait, which was called the Eye of the Needle, and is regarded as the most dangerous stretch of water in the world that became known as the shipwreck coast claiming hundreds of ships that tried to navigate the narrow path between King Island and the southern side of Victoria, Australian mainland. Hence, the term eye of the needle. In good sailing, the distance of over 200 nautical miles could be achieved in one day.

Life at Sea

Life at sea, during 1882 on a sailing vessel, was extremely difficult, to say the least. But for Donald MacLeod and his family, the voyage on the *Renfrewshire* in the southern ocean at the end of winter, conditions would have been terrible. There were wild seas generated by frequent storms, creating the sailing vessel to pitch and roll, waves rising above her on both sides, occasionally crashing onto the ship's deck and water entering the cabins, soaking everything. Lanterns and candles would go out, leaving passengers in the dark soaking wet and cold. Usually ships had three classes. The steerage (the lowest deck and below the water line) was the cheapest and the most uncomfortable. There's lack of ventilation and no portholes that allowed views or lighting. In the steerage, candles or lanterns were sometimes forbidden. Passengers would endure overcrowded and cramped conditions for ninety days or longer. People in 1882 lacked simple hygiene; toilet paper had not been invented, rags where soaked in vinegar and hung on the back of the toilet door to be used by all. This led to diseases like dysentery. Some ships had outbreaks of influenza and tuberculosis that had been brought aboard by other passengers, undetected at medical checks.

Sailors would harpoon dolphins that followed the sailing vessel; dolphin meat was known as sea hog that supplemented their salted meat diet. Birds would be caught by fishing lines, albatrosses' where a prized catch, their skins could be sold in London to make muffins, the winged bones where used to make smoking pipes and the webbed footing where used to make tobacco pouches. On this none stop voyage passengers would entertain themselves with singing, card playing, reading and Church services were also held on the voyage. Navigation of the Renfrewshire to Australia was a complex task that required great skill by the captain, with the use of various navigation tools. They included the telescope, Compass, ship's log and sextant. The captain needed to have knowledge of the position of the stars while sailing at night.

Donald MacLeod and his family arrived at Bunderberg Port, Queensland, Australia, on the 14th of September 1882. The Renfrewshire was to continue making the same journey on the Great Circle for another six years. It was last seen on the 2nd of July 1888 by the steamer Aconcagua, having left Glasgow to sail to Brisbane at Latitude 17'S Longitude 38'W. It was never seen again, together with eighteen people lost to the sea.

CHAPTER EIGHT

Peter MacLeod (alias - Daniel john Livingston MacLeod)
1866–1900 - Mad Woman Christy - The Depression Years 1890s

Peter MacLeod (alias Daniel
John Livingston MacLeod)
1866–1900

The family arrived in Bunderberg, Queensland, Australia, in 1882, to a colony of the then British Empire; now the family was living on foreign soil and in a land of non-Gaelic speaking people. Australia had experienced a gold rush from the 1860s that made Melbourne the wealthiest city in the world. Railways were opening up in the country, and the establishments of large pastoral estates of sheep and cattle were being introduced into the inland. Peter, my great-grandfather, obtained work on the Queensland railway. Donald, being a master blacksmith, would have been able to gain employment in the growing economy as a blacksmith. The two girls, Flora and Maggie, were schooled in Bunderberg and remained there, eventually both marrying and living in the Bunderberg community the rest of their lives.

Mad Woman Christy

Donald's second wife Christy was committed to the Bunderberg asylum for the insane, at Goodna. The records as follows are disturbing, to say the least:

> 'A blue-eyed, brown-haired wrinkled woman with a good deal of hair on her chin there is an old scar across her throat which she says was done with a razor. Bodily organs appear healthy. She talks little English but is very voluble in Gaelic. She is lively but good tempered as a rule recurring she becomes excited violent and tears her dress. She eats well but sleeps poorly. & lively but very jealous in her behaviour July 15 Occasionally violent and noisy at night disturbing her fellows in the dormitory. Aug 18 The same. Sep 24 ?? Oct 18 ?????'

Admitted Documentation June 2, 1893

Rusking about the streets abusing the passers-by, wandered about in her nightdress.

Nov 4- She died at 3.20 this morning
Cause of Death: Dysentery

.... 50	Form of Mental Disorder ....Mania
.............Married	Duration of Attack.......................Years
Wife of Labourer	
Scotland	Date of discharge..............Died Nov 4 1893

Poor Christy McLeod, one's mind boggles how she had her throat cut. Was it an incident on the Isle of Raasay? Had she been suffering from a mental illness all her life? Was it caused from trauma of the past?

Peter, her stepson, had moved away before her admission, and moved to Footscray in Melbourne where he met and married Ann

George. It was when he moved to Melbourne that he went under the alias Daniel John Livingstone McLeod. Donald, his father, had also moved away, gold mining and trying his luck on the gold field at Monal. Father went north and son went south. The authorities had been trying to get Donald to fund the hospitalization of his wife Christy. Letter from Donald that was penned by a JP is as follows:

Police of Bunderberg informing Asylum

> *To Gibson Jackson Esq*
> *Deputy Curator of Insanity*
> *Goodna, Brisbane*
>
> *Sir,*
>
> *Your favour of 27 June '93 to hand re Christy McLeod a patient in the Asylum for the Insane at Goodna. At present I am not in the position to pay any sum of money in support of me above for the last [2] years through lack of employment. I have barely made sufficient money to provide my daily bread. I am considerably advanced in years and have no means of support, except through labour. It is almost impossible for a man at my time of life to get employment at present but should fortune favour I shall be very willing indeed to contribute towards my unfortunate wife's position.*
>
> > *I remain*
> > *Dear Sir*
> > *Yours Truly*
> > *Donald McLeod*
>
> *PS My wife has no relatives except myself in the colony.*
>
> *The above named Donald MacLeod is personally known to me and I believe his statement to be true.*
>
> > *R. P. Clearay J. P.*

It may seem that poor Christy was abandoned by every member of the family, as the authorities of the time would collect payment from the families of the committed. This may be the reason why Peter went under the alias, a young man starting his own family, concerned of the authorities' chasing him for payment of his father's second wife. Other records show a land purchase in the Gladstone region that is near Monal diggings in February 1890 in the name of Donald McLeod, and also another land parcel next door in Peter McLeod's name. All these were forfeited on the 28th January 1893. Another MacLeod, not related, also purchased the land next to Peter and Donald. Records indicate Peter married in Melbourne in 1900, but did work part of the time in Queensland on the railways through the 1890s. It is extremely plausible that this was another reason for Peter's alias: creditors were after him. He was working under Peter McLeod while working in Queensland, but was under the alias Daniel John Livingstone McLeod while living in Melbourne and raising a family. Several branches of the MacLeod Family have all been under the belief there was a fallout, hence, the fabrication of a name. Reason could be that a property deal went sour, and the connection with Peter's family continued with family members in Scotland up until the 1920s. As another descendant to Donald stated, it seems Peter was only hiding from authorities not his family.

Even if the original story was correct that he disowned his father therefore fabricating a new name, then one can understand how hard a life both the father and son had endured. All sharing a little room together in Portree on the Isle of Skye, losing his mother when he was only a small boy. Peter apprenticed to his blacksmith father, spending every day in a small blacksmith shop with him, and again sharing a small room with his stepmother and sisters. Donald must have been a hard man by virtue of the environment he was brought up in, the Highland Clearance of his people, and possibly time in the American Civil War. Both father and son sailing over the sea confined in a small cabin together, stepmother suffering from mania living with him for years, there is an understanding of a possible reason for the possible fallout, and the stigma that went with mental illness at the time. Donald and Peter both would have been hard men by virtue of their life experience and environment not equipped with an understanding of mental illness.

Peter MacLeod lived in a blue stone house in Wearing street Footscray, his wife Ann George had already lived with her parents in the same street. They had five children all born at the Wearing Street address. Janet was born in 1890; Ellen, in 1892; Annie, in 1895. John (Jack), my grandfather, was born in 1897, and another daughter Emma was born in 1899.

Depression Years 1890s

In 1890, the economic rise and prosperity boom that Australia experienced came to an end, and the country was to experience the most severe depression within its history, known as The Great Crash. That was going to last a decade. In 1890 to 1893, the Depression caused the closure and the collapse of many banks. The federal bank ran out of money and closed in April 1893. The Commercial Bank of Australia suspended its operations; twelve other banks soon followed. Pastoralists, businessmen, and land speculators weren't able to pay loans, and thousands of investors were ruined. This caused high unemployment, where literally thousands of men would travel from property to property in search of work. Employers lowered wages. Unions were formed and responded by strike action. The year 1890 saw the Great Maritime Strike; 1891 saw the Australian Shearers' strike followed by a miners' strike. Donald and Peter had left the hardships of the Isle of Skye, and now were experiencing hardships on foreign soil, hence, the reason was necessity to move on looking for work. Peter (alias Daniel) was working in both Melbourne and Queensland railways when work was available, and poor Donald tried to separate gold from clay on the diminishing gold fields. This depression, where thousands of people experienced hunger, gave another reason for Peter's alias to protect what he had: a home with a young family. This was the era when Australia's finest writers and poets emerged; the likes of Banjo Paterson and Henry Lawson. The poem as follows describes the men of Australia trampling the roads during the depression; it was referred to as travelling the wallaby track, when men would carry their swags in search of work across Australia's outback, as the likes of Donald and Peter in search of work during the Depression.

> *'For time means tucker and tramp you must were the scrubs and plains are wide with seldom a track that a man can trust, or a mountain peak to guide, All day long in the dust and heat – when summer is on the track – with stinted stomachs and blistered feet they carry their swags Out back.'*
>
> *—Henry Lawson*

CHAPTER NINE

Tragic Death of Peter MacLeod 1900

While Donald continued his luck mining, he went from Monal gold diggings in the Gladstone region to working on Landsborough Downs in Northern Queensland, on a large sheep station where most likely his master blacksmith kills were in demand. Donald later travelled farther north to the tin mining area at Herberton, in the tropical region of Northern Queensland. The gold boom at Palmer River near Cooktown had petered out, and many miners flocked to the Herberton region to try their luck at tin mining. His son Peter had secured work in Melbourne, and was labouring on a trench site along the railway line at Yarraville on the 14th of March 1900. He was in a trench 2 foot long and 8 foot deep, explosives (gelignite) were being used to loosen the blue stone rock; trains were rattling along the railway line right next to the trench. The walls of the trench collapsed bringing large rocks into the trench, crushing Peter. He was taken to Footscray hospital but died soon after and buried in an unmarked grave within forty hours after his death at Footscray Cemetery.

The coroner's inquest was held on the 16th and 20th of March 1900. Several statements were obtained from his workmates. Outcome was accident? Even though no adequate protection wall was installed, there were very limited safety procedures of the time, and no employer was liable for having this inadequate and dangerous workplace. They sent their employees into blasting explosives in a small trench/shaft then returning to the trench straight after the explosion, to a narrow 2 foot long, 8 foot deep. At the inquest, his workmate John O'Brien states:

> *'I have known him for 5 years, he was a part of the time in Queensland on the railways. He had been on the worked about Melbourne for a good time'*
> — *John O'Brien*

Report on the death of Peter (Daniel John Livingstone) MacLeod [Unreadable some words?]

CRUSHED TO DEATH- AT THE YARRAVILLE SEWERAGE WORKS A few minutes before twelve o'clock on Wednesday morning, an accident of which resulted fatally, occurred at the sewerage works of Messrs Starr Bros, Anderson Street Yarraville, close to the railway gates. The victim was a married man named Daniel McLeod, aged 35, a resident of Wearing Street, Footscray. - The accident: occurred in a cutting, 2 ft long, by ft Ioin wide, and about 8 ft deep; and the debris -discharged from this consisted of clay and bluestone. Between 9 and so o'clock on the morning of the - unfortunate aft there four shots happened put in to remove the stone; and after' the results of the explosion had been removed the surrounding ground appeared 'to be sound. Associated with Mr M'Leod in his work was another labourer, Albeit H. Hansford and immediately before the accident the two men were working within a few feet of one another M'Leod was working in a stooping position while-without the slightest warning, the top and one, of the sides of the cutting above him gave way, completely burying the unfortunate man. Hanford, who escaped very narrowly, gave the alarm and a crowd collected, whilst the?''?opinion tho . . . job immediately set to work to extricate M'Leod. In less than twenty minutes the willing workers succeeded in clearing the earth away but when this was done a pitiable sight met their gaze M'Leod lay face downwards pinned firmly by a huge boulder estimated to weigh about 300 cwt one, cheek resting on another jagged piece of bluestone which further investigation proved had entered his face? During the time the workmen were engaged in extricating the poor fellow, Dri M'Canhy, and Box were sent for and they were on the scene when he was brought to the surface their examination disclosed that the unfortunate sufferer had his right thigh fractured, and the skull seriously injured, in addition to an awful incisor wounded of the: cheek. The medical gentleman dressed the wounds- and did all that was possible then to relieve the patient after which he was removed to the Melbourne: Hospital. 'He was admitted' to that institution b???!-Dr Palmer,' and died about o'clock the same evening . . . The deceased leaves a widow and four children. The 'ganger on the work Mr John O'Brien; states that he visited the place where the accident occurred half an hour before it took place, when everything seemed to be in its normal condition. He did not interfere with' M'Leod whom he believed to be an experienced man. It's estimated that about two tons of earth and stories fell away and it is thought by some that the vibration of the running trains helped to bring the earth down.

Ann McLeod was now widowed with five children to raise the youngest 5 and the oldest 10. She continued to live in the blue stone home in wearing street Footscray raising her brood this is where all her children were born.

To Be Removed From The Public Eye.

Donald MacLeod had travelled further north from the goldfields of Monal in 1893 to 'Landsborough Downs' that is situated near Hughenden in Northern Queensland. Donald most likely gained employment as a master Blacksmith on the large sheep station where his skills would have been needed in cart wheel making, horse shoeing etc. He was hospitalised at Herberton a town further north from Landsborough Downs in the tropical region on the western side of the Atherton tableland. Herberton had become a boom town in the mining of tin, and at one stage the tin was more valuable by weight than gold. The palmer goldfields, north of Herberton had thousands of people converge on this area that included many Chinese miners. Stories of cannibalism emerged where some people reported the Aboriginal people of the area where practising cannibalism that included a story of the eating of some of the Chinese miners. This story has been disputed by many people, but the facts are the story has entered into the Australian folklore being true or false. After the boom of the Palmer Gold fields the gold mining diminished and the majority of the miners, went straight to the new tin mining boom at Herberton. And it was at Herberton, Donald MacLeod was hospitalized only a few weeks after the death of his only son.

The Queensland government at the time had a policy regarding the destitute of the state, all the aged and homeless people, the ones with no money and no assets. The policy was: **'To be removed from the public eye'** This terrible policy applied to the likes of miners, stockman, timber cutters, etc., all the men and women who worked for pittance around the country, now old and arthritic, and unable to work, their crime being poor and were sentenced as an inmate to the Benevolent Asylum Dunwich for the destitute. The asylum was on Stradbroke Island across the water from Brisbane. It was considered a type of haven, and people from across the state of Queensland were rounded up, from settlements, towns, and hospitals, and were taken across the water to the island where they would spend the rest of their lives. This asylum for the destitute was founded in England along the same lines of a poor house, where the policy was to die out of the public eye. The asylum operated from 1864 to 1947. A total of 21,000 people were sent to the island; these were the aged, the infirm, and the destitute, between 1,000 and 1,600 people living there at any one given time. On the death of the person in the asylum, if the family did not claim the body, they would be buried in a pauper's grave, as the likes of Donald MacLeod who died on the 24th of November 1908, at the age of 74 years. He had lived on the island for over eight years since being transported from Herberton in 1900. He was buried in the pauper's grave along with 8,426 other poor souls. It is the largest mass grave in Australia, but is so little known.

The Benevolent Asylum, Dunwich, had been built on Stradbroke Island to house the destitute and aged people of Queensland on the island, east of Brisbane. During Donald's time living there, the accommodation would have been in a calico-type of tent, and meals would have been supplied in a mess hall. Inmates were either housed in calico tent or in a dormitory type of accommodation.

The admission form of the Benevolent Asylum, Dunwich:

Name:	Donald McLeod	Age: 66
When admitted:	May 14th 1900	
Cause of admission:	Bad back arthritic??? [hard to read due to ink pen might be back arthritic]	
Trade or profession:	Blacksmith	
Fathers name:	John McLeod	
Mother's Name:	Ann McCaskill	
Married:	Widowed Ann McCaskill	

History:

Came to Australia 20 years ago, to Bunderberg was here at his trade ...?? and follow north??? 2 years at Bunderberg and Landsborough Downs and Herberton Hospital.

No Money No Property.

Donald, like his forefathers before him, died a pauper, but this time his death certificate does not have the pauper written on it, but his admission to the Destitute Asylum does: "No Money No Assets." This was going to be the last of the family line to be destitute at an old age.

The writer with Wrought Iron gates that were made at Stormy Hill Blacksmith Shop, most likely by Donald or Peter MacLeod 1870s to 1882.

Photo of Anne MacLeod, Donald's daughter, who stayed behind in Scotland, with two Australian soldiers during WW1, 29th battalion badge on arm believed to be Jack MacLeod's mates. From the photo collection of Alan Hawthorn Scotland.

To Gibson Jackson Esq.
Deputy Curator in Insanity
Goodna, Brisbane.

Sir,

Your favor of 27 June/93 to hand re Christina McLeod a patient in the Asylum for the Insane at Goodna. At present I am not in a position to pay any sum of money in support of the above. For the last (2) two years through lack of employment I have barely made sufficient money to provide my daily bread. I am considerably advanced in years and have no means of support except through labour. It is almost impossible for a man at my time of life to get employment at present but should fortune favour I shall be very willing indeed to contribute towards my unfortunate wife's support.

I remain
Dear Sir
Yours truly
Donald McLeod

P.S. My wife has no relatives except myself in the colony

The above named Donald McLeod is personally known to me and I believe his statement to be true.

Letter from Donald MacLeod penned by a J.P Stating he can not afford his daily bread, from the gold diggings Monal Queensland 9th of July 1893.

Only known portrait believed to be of Peter MacLeod
[alias Daniel John Livingstone McLeod].

Voyage on the *Renfrewshire*
by the MacLeod family 1882

Glasgow
Scotland

ATLANTIC
OCEAN

INDIAN
OCEAN

Dumbarton
Australia

Roaring Forties

Equator

The only known photo of the *Renfrewshire*

Chapter Ten

Jack McLeod 1897–1958 - Harry Bliss
MacLeod 1920-1988 - Alistair MacLeod born 1965
- Brandon MacLeod the eighth generation

Jack McLeod
1897–1958

John Henry Bruchmann McLeod, my grandfather, was born in a small blue stone house at 9 Wearing Street, Footscray, in 1897. He was the only son of Peter and Anne. Ironically his grandfather Donald also had only one son as well; Jack himself would only have one son, my father; and I had only one son, Brandon. Five generations of only one son. He was known as Jack (or Macca) and had lost his father when he was a very small child. He had a stepgrandfather Johanna Henry Bruchmann, a Jewish businessman who became a father figure to Jack. Hence, Jack's name was John Henry Bruchmann McLeod named after his stepgrandfather who had married Anne George's widowed mother. It may have been the influence of his Jewish stepgrandfather that assisted Jack to later become a successful businessman.

Watch in family possession inscribed on back:

To J H B McLEOD
On his 15th Birthday
From his Grandfather
J. H. Bruchmann
19.1.12

Jack was born during struggling times, and started boxing in his early teenage years. By the time Jack was 18 years of age, he had had thirty-six boxing fights of which he won thirty-two, two draws, and only two losses. Footscray was known as the pugilist side of town, a very tough area that produced many great boxers over many decades. But Jack's achievement in the boxing ring was to come to an end and another type of fighting was what Jack was to experience with the onset of the first world war. Jack worked in the ammunition factory at Maribynong as well as involved in boxing, and enlisted on the 15th January 1916. He was sent to Broadmeadows for military training then on the 4th of April 1916 embarked at the port of Melbourne on the steam ship *Euripides* bound for Egypt.

They sailed up the Suez Canal to Egypt. Jack as a private number being 2962. From Egypt he was taken to England, Salisbury Plains, in preparation for action in France. In September 1916, Jack was in Estaples, France, and marched in from the 8th Training Brigade. On the 1st of October, he joined the 29th Battalion in the field from the 6th Reinforcements.

Jack's thirty-two boxing fights would have done very little to prepare him for the horrific ordeal he was about to undertake. The 29th Battalion fought on the western front of France and Belgium.

Jack was a signaller who would use a bugle as well as his 303 rifle with bayonet attached. He fought with the 29th Battalion on the last weeks of the Battle of Somme from October to November. Soldiers experienced horrendous conditions living in trenches with once fields of crops now transformed to quagmire. Tens of thousands of horses would be used to cart the heavy artillery and other provisions. The horses would sink and disappear in the mud. Wet and freezing conditions whereby soldiers would experience trench foot due to constantly wet feet. Nearly every soldier would smoke cigarettes to try to stop the stench of decaying corpses that lay everywhere.

The German army used mustard gas that burnt the lungs of their enemy. Jack fought at Polygone Wood after the Battle of Somme and was gassed between the 12th and 27th of September 1917. The next few days, the survivors buried their fallen comrades and the battalion moved to a hill known as Passchendaele. Some of the men who had been fighting for twelve months, like Jack, and longer had been gassed but soldiered on to battle on at Passchendaele, where Australians and their allies where to experience huge casualties. At the battle of Passchendaele, Jack received a gunshot wound to the right thigh and leg. Jack was one of the lucky ones; Australia lost 47,000 soldiers on the western front in France and Belgium. It is believed that over one million people had lost their lives on both sides, including civilians.

Jack was shipped to England where he was hospitalised in Cheltenham, England. It is here he met my grandmother Francis Louisa Maud Bliss who was voluntarily nursing. Maud, as she was called, was from a successful wholesale and retail fruit, poultry, fish, business family that had a large two-story commercial shop in High Street, Cheltenham, England that covered two sites. Jack's service record shows he went AWOL several times as he may have been chasing Nan. But history also tells how many soldiers were not being fed sufficiently in hospitals due to rations and would be fed by local families while recovering from their wounds.

On the 28th of July 1918, Jack had recovered from his wounds and fought in boxing, winning the 3rd Training Brigade Lightweight Championship, collecting a trophy that has been in the family since.

They married on 27th of November 1918, and it is with his war records and marriage certificate that his middle name has been changed from Bruchmann to Buchannan. The reason is not known; he enlisted under Bruchmann and his war medical records along with his marriage certificate show Buchannan, this was most likely a clerical error during the war. All other documentation after the war was back to the Bruchmann middle name.

> '*When I visited Scotland in 2013 Alan Hawthorn who we both share the same great-great-grandfather showed me a photo of his grandmother, Jack's auntie with two Australian soldiers taken in Glasgow they have what seem to be the 29th Battalion badges on their uniforms and Similar faces as from Jack MacLeod's photo collection of the 29th Battalion boys, hence Jacks mates making contact with the MacLeod's of Scotland. He also had a photo of my grandfather Jack taken from Melbourne that his family had kept in there collection for nearly 100 years proving beyond doubt our connection*'

On Jack's return to Australia with his new bride Francis Louise Maude nee Bliss, they moved back to Wearing Street, Footscray, and bought a weather board home at 5 Wearing Street, Footscray, a stone's throw from where Jack was born, but not before his son Harry was born in 1920 in the same blue stone building as his father. Jack and Maude over the years went into several business ventures, the biggest being Jack MacLeod's boxing gymnasium, where he trained many successful fighters, including some that would take Australian titles with the likes of Alan Basten, an Australian middleweight title holder, and Frankie Flannery, an Australian lightweight title holder. Today not a house remains in this street and the street itself has now become Farnsworth Avenue. Jack and Maude created a fish-and-chip business on the corner of Droop Street and Ballarat Road. They had several rabbiters working for them during the Depression years. With what was known as ground mutton, they feed the homeless who gathered in large numbers that were living on the banks of the Maribynong River during these tough times. Jack had bought taxis and employed drivers as well as a leather business, making leather boxing equipment.

Jack had close friendships with the likes of John Wren Power without glory fame, (A book written on this colourful businessman), one of Australia's wealthiest businessman who owned Festival hall the boxing stadium of Victoria. He also had friendships with the likes of Author Frank Clune, ex-footscray footballer Norm Ware, and world champion boxer Freddie Cochrane. He would assist in fitness training at his boxing gymnasium with other sporting identities of the likes as legendary jokey Ron Hutchison.

Unfortunately, the fighting game attracts a lot of undesirables, and Footscray in its time has had its share of gangsters. Jack had trained Jack Appleby who unfortunately was gunned down outside a shoe store in Footscray. Jack would operate a couple of taxis as well as his boxing training and management of fighters. In the 1950s, Jack bought a piece of land overlooking the Maribynong River at Ascot Vale where he built a magnificent Tudor home, which in the day would have been one of the prestigious homes built in the area known as Whiskey Hill. He affectionately called this home 'Dunvegan' after Dunvegan Castle, the seat of the MacLeod chieftain's in the Isle of Skye. He was known to continue his fighting in the later part of life, this time with the Australian Tax office, where he also was successful in that battle.

Jack died on the 28th of December 1958 at his beloved home 'Dunvegan' Ascot Vale. He was ill from the gassing he received as a teenager while fighting in France forty years prior.

CHAPTER ELEVEN

Harry Bliss MacLeod
1920—1988

My father Harry Bliss MacLeod was born on the 20th of March 1920, in the same blue stone house his father twenty-three years before him was born. He later moved to the weatherboard home at 5 Wearing Street, Footscray, and was raised with the boxing gymnasium next to his home, a hive of activity where boxers would train, sparring in the ring on a daily bases. He recalled the days of long horn cattle still being walked down Ballarat road on their way to the Newmarket sale yard. My father was very fortunate, growing up in the twenties and thirties during the Depression years, due to his father's entrepreneurial skills with several businesses going; most other families were not that fortunate.

My father would tell me that when he was young, the neighbour's son was brought home by the police van having been arrested for stealing shoes. So many kids had to go barefoot as their families could not afford shoes and this child had stolen shoes to support his need. The next morning, the father of the boy who stole the shoes was found hanging in the backyard—he had taken his own life, depressed for not being able to buy shoes for his son.

My father had only one fight; he fought a man called Archie Kempt that ended in a draw. Archie later became an Australian champion. Unfortunately, Archie was killed in the ring during a fight. My father was encouraged by his father to obtain work at the local ordinance factory as he did at the age of 15 years, and he stayed there for an incredible forty-five years, his entire working life. When the second world war broke out, Dad went down to enlist but was knocked back on his enlistment due to being needed with his then skills within the ordinance factory. This became a delight to his father Jack, who had deliberately arranged for his son to work in the ordinance factory when he turned 15 as he did not want his only son to experience the horrors of war as he did.

My father's early years were spent exploring the Maribynong River, by water craft, canoe, or raft that he had built himself. Fishing and shooting were a huge past-time for my father. He would shoot hares and sell them to the Braybrook Hotel, where they would hang the dead animals in the front window. A week later they would still be there with the fur falling off and showing a greenish colour to be used in what was known as jug hare soup, a delicacy in those days.

Harry became a keen fly fisherman and would spend at least two months of every year, fishing and camping throughout the high country of New South Wales and Victoria. It was my father's love of the outdoors that introduced me to appreciate the unique environment of the Australian bush.

After forty-five years of service in the ordinance factory, my father retired to live a life he so wanted full time in a natural area of the Australian bush—trout fishing. Unfortunately, cancer denied him of this, and he was only able to enjoy two years of retirement, passing away on the 18th of March 1988. And it was my father's love of his ancestral history and his desire to find out what had happened to his great-grandfather and to confirm the story handed down to me, that has inspired me to research and write the history of my ancestry.

Alistair John MacLeod
Born 1965

And now to me, the seventh generation of MacLeod's father to son of what I know at this stage. My life has been very fortunate, to say the least, compared to the lives of my ancestors. My adversity in life has been overcome with great prosperity, by virtue of being born an Australian in peaceful and great economic times. In 2009, I wrote the book *Never Die Wondering*, an autobiography of my life's journey, of which the publisher described as follows:

> This book is an incredible Australian story of an ordinary man who has lived an extraordinary life, who has overcome seemingly insurmountable obstacles to succeed in living his dreams and accomplishing his ambitions.
>
> Alistair MacLeod's memoirs is a true story of a man who decided to live life to the full.
>
> You will be enchanted as you follow his adventurous life of travel and living from the city to the remote Snowy Mountains and the Kimberley's just to mention a few.
>
> You will be inspired by his hard work that lead him through the Outback and the city with many roles from Jackeroo, Show time Spruiker, timber miller, tourist Operator, Horseman, Salesmen, Cattlemen, Investor to a successful property developer.
>
> Alistair's story is also one of mateship and the Australian bush, mustering of cattle, pack horse treks, and skiing in the High Country, personal and business triumphs and overcoming the hardships that life dealt along the way.
>
> Fighting droughts, a legal system after he used a firearm in self defence, the injustice of the family law court, the rights of a father and son whilst enduring betrayals both personal and business, are just some of the crashing battles fought in his life.

These battles rendered him penniless in his later part of life.

With his usual never give up attitude he remarkably created a property portfolio in the millions in just 48 months, created from mentors, business minds of millionaires from the bush and the city.

This is an autobiography that every person can identify with at some level. It will inspire and entertain you. It is defiantly not to be missed.

An astonishing book, quite incredible, written with plain spoken humour and succinct insight.

A J MacLeod recalls both jubilant victories and crushing defeats while describing the determined personal and business philosophy that drives his life.

Brandon Alistair MacLeod

The eighth generation

My son Brandon was born on the 26th December 1994 at Wagga Wagga NSW and he had lived on our grazing properties in the Snowy Mountains of Tumbarumba NSW. His child hood was a life on the land working cattle and riding horses. Firstly a 100 acre holding and later living on a 1,000 acre property of which bordered 1.5 million acres of High Country ensuring an adventurous boy hood. In his teen years we moved to Melbourne where he attended school and became a qualified carpenter and gained experience on construction sites as a form worker. He lived in the Maribyrnong valley where five generations of MacLeod's had lived since 1890. As he was growing up I found myself explaining to him of the story my father had told to me when I was a boy, of who he is, a **MacLeod** the Mac meaning Son in Gaelic and the Leod a Norse name derived from the Viking era. A coin handed down through the generations dated 1797. Our Ancestral home was in far western Scotland on the Isle of Skye.

Everyone has a similar story of their family history. Everyone would have some exciting advents in their ancestral bloodline; most people have just not discovered their ancestry history.

This book is our history of who we are, father to son, now eight generations:

Son of a Highlander:

> '*For that is the mark of the Scots of all classes: that he stands in an attitude towards the past unthinkable to Englishmen, and remembers and cherishes the memory of his forebears, good or bad. And there burns alive in him a sense of identity with the dead even to the twentieth generation.*'
>
> **Robert Louis Stevenson**

Across the world, it is estimated that forty million people can claim Scottish heritage, and a large part of these people can contribute the original exodus of their ancestors from their lands, due to the horrendous Highland Clearances.

Alan Hawthorn in Scotland with a photo of my Grandfather Jack MacLeod taken in Melbourne. This photo has been in Alan's family for nearly 100 years proving beyond doubt our family connection.

Jessie MacLeod, who had refused to sail to Australia, on the *Renfrewshire*, here are two of her daughters pictured above

On the photo on the left is Jessie Jnr, on the right Anne with her family, taken in Glasgow from Jack MacLeod's collection.

Minnie Paterson, Jessie's other daughter whom was in correspondence with Jack MacLeod while he was wounded recovering in an English hospital in 1917.

Explanations of who the photos were and addresses all written on the back of the photos.

Signed from your loving cousin Minnie

The steam ship "Euripides" of which left Melbourne port with Jack MacLeod to Egypt during WW1

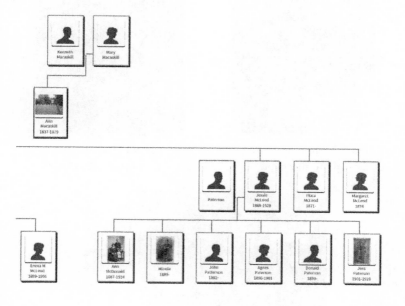

Jack bottom left of the
photo in Egypt.

Jack standing in
center England.

29th Battalion boys in France, Jack in middle with x holding paper.

ABOUT THE AUTHOR

Alistair MacLeod is a third generation Australian born in 1965 of Scottish Highland descent. He is an accomplished author with his first book *Never Die Wondering*, an autobiography of the author's adventurous journey in life while overcoming insurmountable obstacles to succeed in living his dreams and accomplishing his ambitions.

The author has a unique style of storytelling, with his plain spoken humour and succinct insights. His love for history, travel, and culture is evident in his storytelling and comes through in his writing.

Alistair has had many roles throughout his adventurous life. He started his working life as a show time spruiker then as a Jackeroo leaving home as a 17 year old and travelling Outback Australia. As a stockman, he worked on cattle and sheep stations with many itinerate jobs over several years travelling and exploring Australia. Buying his first grazing property at only 23 years of age in the Snowy

Mountains. An entrepreneur who has had many business ventures creating an adventure horse trekking tourist business, developing a value adding timber processing milling operation, purchasing and developing several cattle grazing properties, and many other property development ventures over 30 years.

A Road scholar not a Rhodes scholar, a raconteur whose life experiences and personal and business philosophies that drive his life are emphasised in his writing.

A successful businessman who has made his wealth through property development and Investment, that has enabled the author to explore many parts of the world, listening to stories from others and learning about different cultures and history.

The author lives most of the year on the Victorian coast, where he enjoys sailing his yacht, since retirement from horseback riding, and continues his travelling and exploring to remote locations across Australia and the world.

ORDER A BOOK ON LINE

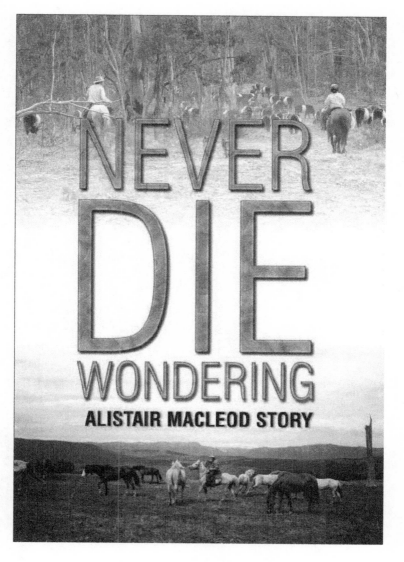

Go to www.neverdiewondering.com.au.

CPSIA information can be obtained
at www.ICGtesting.com
Printed in the USA
BVOW11s0503150617
486945BV00001B/34/P